Forgiveness...
It Is Not
Optional!

Forgiveness... It Is Not Optional!

David LeRoy Childers

XULON PRESS

Xulon Press
2301 Lucien Way #415
Maitland, FL 32751
407.339.4217
www.xulonpress.com

Unless otherwise indicated, Scripture quotations taken from the King James Version (KJV) – *public domain.*

Scripture quotations taken from the Holy Bible, New International Version (NIV). Copyright © 1973, 1978, 1984, 2011 by Biblica, Inc.™. Used by permission. All rights reserved.

Scripture quotations taken from Reina–Valera (RV) Copyright © 1995 by the United Bible Societies. Used by permission. All rights reserved.

Disclaimer:
Some names and identifying details have been changed to protect the privacy of individuals.

I have tried to recreate events, locales and conversations from my memories of them. In order to maintain their anonymity in some instances I have changed the names of individuals and places, I may have changed some identifying characteristics and details such as physical properties, occupations and places of residence

Edited by Xulon Press.

Printed in the United States of America.

ISBN-13: 978-1-54563-099-0

Dedication

I dedicate this book to my loving and wonderful wife Madeline, with whom I have enjoyed over 36 years of marriage. She is the beautiful rose God has placed in my life. She is strong, loving, and very supportive. She encouraged me more than anyone else to write this book. I thank God for her! Any accomplishments I may attain in life should go first to her because she has helped to make me the best version of myself!

I also want to thank my parents, Pastor Paul and Ferle Childers who gave me a spiritual foundation that is worth everything. My mom especially encouraged me to begin studying the subject of forgiveness at age 16.

I am grateful to Loren Cunningham who introduced the forgiveness message to me (plus 5,000 other youth) at a Youth Convention in San Diego, California in 1974, again at the age of 16.

I am grateful to Paul Childers my nephew who challenged and encouraged me to write a book on this subject.

I am thankful to Scott and Marisa Smith who have faithfully encouraged me to minister the forgiveness message in Spain and are totally instrumental in shepherding this book into existence. Without Scott, this book would not have been published.

Finally, to Dr. George Wood, my friend, whose sermons have fallen like a refreshing rain on my soul and spirit....truly a shower of blessing and encouragement from Heaven.

THANK YOU JESUS FOR YOUR TRUTH.....IT SETS US FREE!!!!

Table of Contents

Chapter Seventeen

Chapter Eighteen

Chapter Nineteen

Chapter Twenty

Chapter Twenty-One

Introduction

I t is the nature of God to heal. That is why He does not leave us the way He finds us. God wants us to get healed. This book is dedicated to seeing people get healed by the truth of God and His Word.

In John 8:31-44, we discover, in the words of Jesus, six truths.

1. If we are truly His disciples, then we will listen to what He has to say.
2. Then we will know the truth and the truth will set us free.
3. Who the Son sets free, is free indeed.
4. Satan is a liar and the father of all lies.
5. Satan has no truth in himself.
6. When Satan speaks in his native language, it is the language of lies.

In this passage, Jesus reveals the truth about Himself, His power, and His purpose. Jesus also gives us significant insight into the power of Satan: who he is, what he does, and how his kingdom of darkness operates against Christians. Remember the words of Paul the Apostle: "We wrestle not against flesh and blood, but against powers and principalities, and spiritual wickedness in high places" (Ephesians 6:12). The number one power of Satan and demons is their lies.

If a demon's lie becomes our truth, then that area of our life becomes destroyed and remains unhealed. Put enough lies together from demons, that we accept as our truth, and we will end up with destroyed, unhealed, and hurting lives. I am dedicated to seeing you set free and healed by the truth of Jesus. Because who the Son sets free, is free indeed.

Forgiveness Prayer **Model**

1. In the name of Jesus Christ, I choose to forgive (<u>name of person</u>) for (<u>list offense(s)</u>).
2. I don't feel like forgiving (<u>name of person</u>), but I choose to do so out of obedience to Jesus Christ.
3. I choose to forgive by my will because the Lord wants me to and I want to be more like Christ in every way!
4. I understand that I forgive for Christ, not because (<u>name of person</u>) deserves it or wants it.
5. Since I am choosing to forgive, I affirm that (<u>name of person</u>) did hurt me. He/She/They are guilty of hurting me, but through Christ, I choose to forgive him/her/them. In the name of Jesus Christ, I pray this prayer. Amen!

Blessings in Christ,
David Childers

Biblical Forgiveness

Understanding and Practicing Biblical Forgiveness

Many Christians gain spiritual breakthroughs and even deliverance in different areas of their lives. Unfortunately, many times, they do not keep these wonderful victories in Christ. The main reason people cannot keep their spiritual victories, healings, and deliverances is because they have not forgiven someone (or a group) who has hurt/brutalized them. Un-forgiveness is a major obstacle to maturity and a major component of remaining unhealed. So let's learn to forgive so we can live in freedom, spiritual power, and authority.

The Greek word for forgiveness is *aphieme*, which means, "to release." When we forgive someone, or ourselves, we are choosing "to release" the individual in our emotions and in our minds for what they did to us. We release our offender from our hate, bitterness, and resentment. We release them to God. He will pay them back!

Chapter One

What Happens if We Choose Not to Forgive?

We are Not Forgiven of Our Sins

The simple but profound truth of the Lord's Prayer is this: If we do not forgive people who have offended and/or brutalized us, then we will not be forgiven of our sins by God the Father. Let us read Matthew 6:9-15:

> This, then, is how you should pray: "Our Father in heaven, hallowed be your name, your kingdom come, your will be done, on earth as it is in heaven. Give us today our daily bread. And forgive us our debts, as we also have forgiven our debtors. And lead us not into temptation but deliver us from the evil one."

The Lord's Prayer shows the practice of forgiveness should already be established in our lives.

"Forgive us our debts," means to forgive us of our sins. Sin is a debt we owe God. Jesus goes on to say, "As we also have forgiven our debtors." In other words, we should already have forgiven those who owe us because they have offended or brutalized us. From Christ's point of view, forgiving others is the only acceptable lifestyle for the Christian.

Therefore, we need a new phrase to use in our life, "The Lifestyle of Forgiveness." Jesus presupposes that forgiving others is the lifestyle of the Christian walk. The Lord knows this idea of forgiveness is so shocking and unbelievably hard for those born with a sin nature in a fallen world, that He adds two additional statements with emphasis for further understanding to support the radically crazy idea of forgiving those who have hurt us.

Look at verses 14 and 15: "For if you forgive men when they sin against you, your heavenly Father will forgive you. But if you do not forgive men their sins, your Father will not forgive your sins."

What is Jesus saying here? He is speaking plainly: if we refuse to forgive others, then God the Father will not forgive our sins. If our sins remain un-forgiven, how do we plan to get into heaven? How does an un-forgiven sinner (someone whose sins are still attached to them and not removed) get into heaven? Sin cannot enter heaven. Jesus does not come out and say it, but there is no room in heaven for an unforgiving Christian! He plainly states the truth about how the Father views un-forgiveness. It leads to the conclusion that our eternity is plainly in jeopardy. Is un-forgiveness the sin that will keep you out of heaven? The hurt, offense, or brutalization that you have suffered can raise its ugly head again by preventing you from entering heaven. We need to be people who choose to forgive and avoid being eternally victimized by an offender. Don't let your offender and your un-forgiveness destroy your life and your eternal life. Remember, there is no room in heaven for an unforgiving Christian.

Chapter Two

If We Don't Forgive . . .

Demons Have Scriptural Grounds to Torture and Torment Us

I f we don't forgive, demons have Scriptural grounds to torture and torment us emotionally and mentally, which may also lead to physical illness or even death!

The kingdom of Satan and his emissaries (demons) have to engage us based upon the rules established by God. Jesus lets us in on a great spiritual truth of which demons are much aware! It is found in the parable of the un-forgiving, forgiven servant in Matthew 18:21-35. The spiritual laws found in this passage give the forces of Satan power to wreak havoc in the lives of those who do not forgive.

> Then Peter came to Jesus and asked, "Lord, how many times shall I forgive my brother when he sins against me? Up to seven times?" Jesus answered, "I tell you, not seven times, but seventy-seven times." Therefore, the kingdom of heaven is like a king who wanted to settle accounts with his servants. As he began the settlement, a man who owed him ten thousand talents was brought to him. Since he was not able to pay, the master ordered that he and his wife and his children and all that he had be sold to repay the debt. The servant fell on his knees before

him. "Be patient with me," he begged, "and I will pay back everything." The servant's master took pity on him, canceled the debt and let him go. But when that servant went out, he found one of his fellow servants who owed him a hundred denarii. He grabbed him and began to choke him. "Pay back what you owe me!" he demanded. His fellow servant fell to his knees and begged him, "Be patient with me, and I will pay you back." But he refused. Instead, he went off and had the man thrown into prison until he could pay the debt. When the other servants saw what had happened, they were greatly distressed and went and told their master everything that had happened. Then the master called the servant in. "You wicked servant," he said, "I canceled all the debt of yours because you begged me to. Shouldn't you have had mercy on your fellow servant just as I had on you?" In anger, his master turned him over to the jailers to be tortured, until he should pay back all he owed. "This is how my heavenly Father will treat each of you unless you forgive your brother from your heart."

Let's take a closer look at a few verses, starting with verse 21. Peter is trying to appear spiritual. Rabbinical law stated if you forgave someone three times, you're spiritual or mature. Peter doubled it and added one (perhaps because the number seven is a godly number). Remember, the disciples were always trying to figure out who was the greatest in their group. (In the Greek, Jesus constantly referred to his disciples as "little faiths." Hey, "little faiths" let's go here or hey, "little faiths," do that.) There was a great contest between the disciples as to who was the greatest next to Jesus. Jesus is unimpressed by Peter but uses the occasion to teach on forgiving those who hurt and offend us.

In verse 22, Jesus answers, "not seven times, but seventy-seven times." In the King James Version, it is 7x70, or 490 times. With these words, Jesus is revealing a great spiritual truth that forgiveness is the only response true believers can have to a hurt or an offense. Forgiveness is unlimited and also ongoing. Jesus is saying to His followers that we must forgive. Period. End of discussion.

In verses 23-35, Jesus reveals important truths about the forces of darkness. In the story, the servant who owed the king was forgiven $176,800,000, which was too much to pay back. The king, in the Greek, was "filled with tenderness and forgave the loan." The forgiven servant goes out and finds a guy who owes him a few dollars and demands payment in full. He refuses to forgive his fellow servant of such a menial debt and even has him thrown into jail. He had just been forgiven a debt he could never repay! He had a double standard. He wanted to be forgiven but did not want to forgive others. The king finds out about it and in anger, takes the un-forgiving forgiven servant with the double standard and turns him over to the jailer to be tortured.

Let's examine the principles in the parable. The King is Jesus. The enormous debt that is owed is our sin. The first servant is you and me. We owe God a huge debt because we are sinners. We have no way to pay for our sin except with our own death. The second servant represents others who have hurt us. Even though their offense against us may be great, when compared to what we owe Jesus, it is a much smaller amount. The jailer is Satan and the demons that do his bidding.

In this parable, it is revealed demons have Scriptural grounds to torture and torment us emotionally and mentally. Our un-forgiveness grants them the power to do this. Not forgiving others gives demons unfettered power to bring a plethora of negative emotions to crush us: hurt, fear, hate, bitterness, feelings of loneliness, feeling unloved, feelings of little or no worth, etc. If you have been hurt in life, and have not forgiven the person that offended you, then you are already well acquainted with the emotional and mental torment that is in your life. You are experiencing it firsthand. You are being battered around by demons because un-forgiveness is ruling in your life. Demons have power and authority to torture and torment you as long as you refuse to forgive—or don't know how to forgive—those who have hurt you.

Let's review. If we don't forgive, then:

- We are not forgiven of our sin. This prevents us from going to heaven.
- Demons have Scriptural grounds to torture us emotionally, mentally, and physically.

The consequences for not forgiving are terrible and it gets worse. There are more negative things that will happen to us if we cling to un-forgiveness.

Chapter Three

If We Don't Forgive . . .

We Become Like the Person We Don't Forgive

If we don't forgive, we will become like the person we don't forgive in the area of negative character and personality traits. God's Word is clear about what we set before our mind to dwell upon. The King James Version of Proverbs 23:7 reads, "As a man thinketh in his heart, so is he." Many would say this verse is used to teach that you become like—or a product of—your thinking. And they would be right.

The NIV footnote reads similarly, "For as he thinks within himself, so he is." When someone hurts or brutalizes you, if you won't forgive, you set up a movie in your mind of the event and emotions that go with it. The movie is on a loop and it plays over and over. It becomes the issue upon which you dwell. It is what you set before your mind and emotions and you become like that person. Many times I have had pastoral care sessions with people who have become like the person who has hurt them. Many pedophiles that were molested as children or were on the receiving end of violence in the form of emotional, mental, and physical abuse ended up becoming like the person that brutalized them. A large percentage of alcoholics were raised by one or both parents who were alcoholics. As a child, they vowed never to touch alcohol. Yet, they became like the person that was neglectful, AWOL, or abusive because they were consumed by alcoholism.

You have probably heard the phrase "hurt people, hurt people" and that is true. I would add, "Healed people help others to become healed." God wants more healed people because they have opportunity to become people of maturity. Jesus wants us to become healed and mature so we can help others gain their healing.

Many times I have encountered people who marry an individual who is like the parent who hurt them or the one they got along with the least. Living in un-forgiveness reaches out in many directions in our lives.

This idea is supported by Paul as he writes in Philippians 4:8, "Finally, brothers and sisters, whatever is right, whatever is pure, whatever is lovely, whatever is admirable—if anything is excellent or praiseworthy—think about such things." Forgiving our offenders gives us the ability to become a right thinker. Living in an unforgiving state cripples us from performing this verse in our lives. We have not released our offender (and the offense) through forgiveness; thus, we have not been released to right thinking and to that point we become like the person we don't forgive. May God help us to start forgiving so we can become healed and then help others find their healing.

Let's review. If we don't forgive, then:
- We are not forgiven of our sins! This prevents us from going to heaven.
- Demons have Scriptural grounds to torture and torment us.
- We become like the person we don't forgive.

Chapter Four

If We Don't Forgive . . .

We Live in Disobedience and Remove Ourselves from Divine Protection and Peace

Scott Smith, a missionary in Spain, said he believes forgiving is the hardest thing God calls Christians to do.

Many times people want to know the biblical alternative to forgiveness. Forgiveness is so distasteful, people question what other options are available to them. There are none! Living in un-forgiveness is disobedience, and therefore, it is sin. Forgiveness is a command. If we ignore it or refuse it, we are inviting disaster into our lives. Many times people bury the offense/hurt/brutalization in their lives believing that is the answer. It is not. They think, *If I just don't think about it, it will go away.* We cannot wish hurts away. When we are hurt, we must choose to address the issue through forgiveness so we can be healed. When we bury an offense, it becomes a coping mechanism, but it does not bring healing. As we grow in Christ, because it is His nature to heal, He eventually forces it back to the surface of our lives so that we can get healed.

People will say, "Well, I have no one I need to forgive."

I always respond, "Oh, really? Let's ask God to bring it back to your memory."

I am no longer surprised by the number of issues and events people begin to remember. What is usually hiding in our buried hurts is the nine-year-old child that is still wounded (you fill in the age).

I dealt with a young woman during a biblical forgiveness care session. We talked about her hurts from her mom. I asked her if her mom had spoken hurtful words to her. She said no. I asked if she had been physically or verbally abusive. She again answered no. As we talked a little bit more, I discovered she had buried the truth. It came to light that her mother had called her a "bit**," a "piece of sh**," and a "sl**." And her mother was a Christian! She said these things in anger. That is why we don't act on our anger.

Dear Christian friends, do not use vulgarities on anyone, especially your children. I am finding this practice is too common among Christian families. When parents say these things, they become deep hurts in a child's psyche. This young woman had buried these events because they were too painful with which to deal. Yet, this toxic hurt began to influence her life negatively because that's what these types of hurts do.

I asked her, "Why did you tell me your mom had not said hurtful words to you when, in fact, she had?"

She froze and began to cry. She said she didn't know why she said the opposite of truth. Part of the reason is she did not want to have to face the pain of the hurt; secondly, she felt she was dishonoring her mother by speaking the truth; thirdly, when her mother said those hateful words and degrading statements, it reminded her of feeling unloved and of having little or no value; and fourthly, pride enters into it. When we factor these four things: 1) pride, 2) emotional pain, 3) dishonoring parents, and 4) feeling unloved and of no value, there is great impetus to not tell the truth. If we don't tell the truth, however, we can never get healed. The truth sets us free. I led her in the *Forgiveness Prayer* three times. She said it out loud. I said it and she would repeat it.

Forgiveness Prayer

1. In the name of Jesus Christ, I choose to forgive (<u>name of person</u>) for (<u>list offense(s)</u>).
2. I don't feel like forgiving (<u>name of person</u>), but I choose to do so out of obedience to Jesus Christ.
3. I choose to forgive by my will because the Lord wants me to and I want to be more like Christ in every way!
4. I understand I forgive for Christ, not because (<u>name of person</u>) deserves it or wants it.
5. Since I am choosing to forgive, I affirm (<u>name of person</u>) did hurt me. He/She/They are guilty of hurting me, but through Christ I choose to forgive him/her/them. In the name of Christ, I pray this prayer. Amen!

By choosing to forgive, she began to realign herself with Jesus and began to enjoy His divine protection. When we do that, we experience His peace. She sensed His peace come over her. If we don't forgive, we live in our disobedience and remove ourselves from divine protection and peace.

Let's review. If we don't forgive, then:
- We are not forgiven of our sins.
- Demons have Scriptural grounds to torture and torment us.
- We become like the person we don't forgive.
- We live in disobedience and remove ourselves from divine protection and peace.

Chapter Five

If We Don't Forgive . . .

We Try to Get Revenge and Revenge is Wrong

I f un-forgiveness is the father of our lives, then its child is revenge. Many people believe that revenge will bring them sweet satisfaction. It is rarely accomplished. When revenge is attained, it usually does not bring the results for which we are looking. Revenge typically does not live up to our hopes and dreams. That is because when we try to exact revenge, we are stealing from God. God says emphatically in Romans 12:19 and Deuteronomy 32:35 "Vengeance belongs to the Lord, I will repay." Who owns repayment? Who owns payback? God does!

Paul writes in his letter to the church at Rome: "Do not take revenge, my friends, but leave room for God's wrath, for it is written: 'It is mine to avenge; I will repay,' says the Lord" (Romans 12:19).

Paul takes this from Deuteronomy 32:35: "It is mine to avenge; I will repay. In due time their foot will slip; their day of disaster is near and their doom rushes upon them." If we don't forgive, we attempt to make people pay for their injury to us, and this violates the Scripture. God does not allow revenge to bring about the results we want because He does not want us stealing what He states belongs to Him. Some people believe God is using them as His instrument of vengeance and they can share in His payback. God does not need your help. He is God. Repeat this to yourself three times: "God does not need my help."

Finally, some people don't want God to payback because they're afraid He won't be hard enough! This is a double standard. We want God to be gentle to us when we do wrong and harsh to those who do us wrong. Stop worrying about whether or not God will be hard enough on them. Instead, be thankful for the mercy and kindness He has shown to you.

There is a story of a woman in Texas who tried to get revenge on her stepdaughter. One day, she called her pastor to explain she was sick and tired of her stepdaughter, who, as a teenager, had given birth to a child out of wedlock. She had concealed the pregnancy for months. The teenager, who then had a baby, had done something wrong in regard to the household chores. The stepmother had built up a general hatred and resentment toward her stepdaughter for the deception, cost, and aggravation of the entire situation. This Christian woman's response (because of un-forgiveness) was to kick her stepdaughter and grandchild out on the streets.

It seems the girl's father, even though he lived in the home, paid the bills, and was in authority, had little to say in the matter. When the enraged stepmother called her pastor, she said that she wanted the girl and the baby to live on the streets. She wanted the girl's life to be destroyed and she wanted her to feel pain and misery. When the woman's pastor rebuked her vengeful un-Christian attitude, she would not submit to his correction. When another family in the church took the teenager and baby into their home, the stepmother's family left the church. They strongly disapproved of the rescuing family's desire to save the teenager and baby from the streets.

The power of un-forgiveness and revenge can become the spiritual nuclear power generated for destruction. The destroyed life this woman had wished upon her stepdaughter was visited upon her and her husband's youngest daughter, the biological daughter she loved. This daughter left home as an angry teenager, and became homeless for a while. She got involved in drug addiction and a devastatingly immoral lifestyle and was even in and out of mental hospitals.

If we don't forgive, we may try to get revenge. God says revenge belongs to Him. Be wary of the negative things you want visited upon others. Un-forgiveness may bring destruction on our own loved ones as we attempt to realize our revenge.

Let's review. If we don't forgive, then:

- We are not forgiven of our sins! This prevents us from going to heaven.
- Demons have Scriptural grounds to torture and torment us.
- We become like the person we don't forgive.
- We live in disobedience and remove ourselves from divine protection and peace.
- We try to get revenge, and revenge is wrong.

Chapter Six

If We Don't Forgive . . .

We End Up in Prison!

I f we don't forgive (release), we keep offenders in "our little prison," or so we think. We turn around and realize instead of the prison bars surrounding our offender, the bars are surrounding us. We are in the prison of un-forgiveness, bitterness, resentment, hate, fear, and murder. All these negative emotions lead to our own spiritual death and may also lead to our physical death. Any medical practitioner will attest to the devastating stress that comes from not forgiving. Does the kingdom of darkness have you in prison through un-forgiveness? There is only one way out of this prison. The evil one wants to destroy your life and your eternal life. He will use not forgiving those who have hurt and brutalized you to do it.

I am thinking of a man who, years ago, went to Africa as a missionary. He had his wife and young son with him. They went into the heart of Africa. His wife was expecting a second child, and they were in a remote area. The people they went to share the gospel with did not want to receive them, and village after village refused them hospitality. His wife became ill with malaria. Finally, they had traveled as far as they could. She had no strength left, so he begged the village chief to let him stay in that village.

"At least let me stay until my child is born," he pleaded.

"You cannot live in the village, but you can live on top of that hill," the chief said.

There was a small hill outside of the village. He put a shelter there. The chief forbade anyone to talk to this man and his wife, with one exception. Every day, a ten-year-old boy brought them food. He delivered vegetables, grain, chicken, and eggs. Every day this ill mother would witness to him about Jesus Christ. There came a day when this little ten-year-old boy knelt and gave his life to Jesus Christ. This dear missionary's wife put her arms around him and led him in a confession of faith to receive Jesus as his Lord and Savior.

Shortly after that, the mother gave birth to a baby girl a number of weeks premature. She was sickly and underweight, and she looked like she would die. Yet, the mother died first. Within a matter of hours of giving birth to her daughter, this missionary's wife died. This father became bitter; he blamed God for what happened and sank into despair.

He said to the Lord, "I came to Africa. I learned a foreign language. I wanted to win people to Jesus Christ, and we haven't won anybody to Jesus Christ. Now, I've lost my wife, and my little girl isn't even expected to live." So he said, "I'm going back home." His home was in Europe.

He thought, *I'm no longer going to be a missionary. I'm not going to even be a Christian anymore. I'm not going to live for Jesus.* So he set off to leave. His little baby girl was given to different African women to feed. But they were hundreds of miles from the coast where he could catch a ship. He had some friends who were missionaries. They sought to comfort him, but he refused. "I'm going home," he said.

"Well, if you're going home, that little girl is too sick to travel," they said. "You will have to leave her here."

He agreed, "Okay. I will leave her with you. You bring her to me when you can," and he left his daughter.

Now the reason I tell you this story is because that little girl grew up. She became friends of a minister that I know who shared this story in one of his sermons in Las Vegas, Nevada.

The baby girl never made it to her father in Europe. Instead, she was brought to America. Her father lost all interest in her. He became a bitter man. He became an alcoholic. He was a heavy smoker. He never went to church, and he cursed the name of Christ. Many years went by. The little girl grew up and married a minister. Her husband became president of a Christian college.

Then, on their twenty-fifth anniversary, the college gave them an anniversary gift. The gift was a trip to go to the city in which her father lived. She wrote a letter to her father whom she had never met! After a number of weeks, an answer came back. "I would like to meet you." So she prepared to go. On the day she was scheduled to leave, she went outside to get the mail. In the mail was a news-paper written in a foreign language, her father's language.

She thought, *What is this? I've never seen this before.* Immediately, she took the newspaper to a college friend who knew the language. As she looked through the pages of the magazine, she saw a picture. It was a picture of a hill. At the bottom of the hill was a white wooden cross. The cross was a marker on a grave and the caption on the photograph identified the grave as the grave of her mother. She had never seen a picture of her mother's grave. So she got the story interpreted.

Later that day, she got onto the plane to go to Europe. Her brother, whom she had never met, who was only two years old when she born, met her at the airport.

He said, "Father has had a stroke and he is unable to meet you this evening, but he is looking forward to meeting you tomorrow. He has one request to make of you, and that is that you do not mention the name of Jesus when you see him. He knows you are a Christian, and he knows you are a minister's wife."

She didn't say anything to this request. The next day, she went to her father's home. It was evident when she walked in that she was in the home of an alcoholic. Bottles of liquor were everywhere. The heavy smell of cigarette smoke was in the house. She went into his bedroom. There he lay, with part of his body paralyzed from the stroke. She was about fifty years old and had never met her father. They fell into each other's arms and wept. After a while, they began to talk. In the course of the conversation, she mentioned the name Jesus.

Immediately, he raised his hand and said, "Stop."

She said to him, "Oh, Father! After all these years, you have thought God failed you. All these years, you have lived with blame. All these years, you have lived with despair. You thought that nothing happened in your ministry in Africa. You thought God let you down." Then she pulled the newspaper out of her purse. She said, "Father, do you see this? This is the picture of Mama's grave, and it tells the story of what happened. Do you remember the ten-year-old boy Mama led to the Lord? Well, he grew up. He kept his Christian faith. He went off to college! He learned to become a schoolteacher. He came back to his village. He taught all the village children in school and he led every single child to faith in Jesus Christ. He led every single parent to faith in Jesus Christ. Every single person in that village of six hundred people came to Jesus Christ, including the village chief!

"Oh, see father, it was not in vain!"

He began to weep. All that time he thought God had abandoned him. He came through to a new faith in the Lord Jesus Christ that day.

Several years later, this same woman went to a large conference in London, England. Thousands of people were at the conference, and she was in the back of the auditorium. On the platform were various ministers from many countries. She noticed as a short African man was introduced as the head of a 110,000 member church. The Holy Spirit said within her, "Talk to that man after the service."

After the service, she and her husband made their way to him. She entered the conversation of a small group of people around him, and asked him, "Did you ever hear of ...? She told him the names of her parents. He became real still and looked at her. "Why do you ask?" he responded.

"Because I am their daughter." Suddenly, he let out a tremendous cry from the inner most being of his belly. He picked her up and began to dance around in a circle. He was both laughing and crying. Finally, he explained his joy. "I am the little boy your mother led to Jesus Christ." He had now become the leader of 110,000 Christians.

What the devil wants to do is to take the hard times in our life and defeat us. He wants to fill us with blame, despair, hopelessness, and cause us to give up. The day of triumph was established that day when the missionary's wife led that ten-year-old boy to Jesus Christ. In his darkest hour, when the mother had died, it appeared God was not good, loving, or faithful. Yet, God was still good, loving, and faithful. He needed to persevere in God in order to know this truth. In your darkest hour, God is good, loving, and faithful. Persevere in order to see this truth.

If you feel God has failed you in life's darkest hour, He hasn't. He is working from an eternal perspective. So, if you need to forgive God because you believe God has let you down, it's okay. God understands our human perspective.

Let's review. If we don't forgive, then:
- We are not forgiven of our sins! This prevents us from going to heaven.
- Demons have Scriptural grounds to torture and torment us.
- We become like the person we don't forgive.
- We live in disobedience and remove ourselves from divine protection and peace.
- We try to get revenge and revenge is wrong.
- We end up in the prison we built for our offender.

Chapter Seven

If We Don't Forgive ...

We Limit the Ministry God Has for Us!

Years ago, an older minister who had deeply hurt my parents and by extension, myself, came to me and asked me for help. He said he had a problem and it was an extreme issue in his life. (It was not about immorality.) He said God spoke to him that I was the only one who could help him. We met for breakfast and he related to me the problem. I was shocked God wanted me to minister to this respected pastor. As he described his situation, the Lord spoke to me about how I could help him in spiritual warfare. As I shared with him, the Holy Spirit spoke to me. He said, "David, would you be able to minister to him if you had not forgiven him for hurting your family?" Of course not. Then He spoke to me about this truth. If we don't forgive, we limit the ministry God has for us. The pastor later recounted to me that what I had shared with him worked. Praise God! It is great when you get to be the glove into which God inserts His hand to help others overcome their problems. But the greater insight for me was that forgiveness powerfully creates a whole new level in which God wants us to live. If I had not forgiven this brother, then I would not have been in a position to minister to him. Forgiveness releases us to new levels of ministry that we otherwise would not be able to attain. The same is even true for our Lord and Savior Jesus Christ.

Just imagine for a moment that Jesus, when hanging on the cross, decided what was happening to Him was unfair. He was sinless, perfect, and without a sin nature. He was the only one in the history of the world that would not have to pay for the wage of sin. Yet the Father wanted him to sacrifice His life for a bunch of ingrates who didn't care about God, or law, or the truth. All they cared about was themselves. What if Jesus decides He doesn't want to forgive us. He doesn't want to play out the card of injustice that was the will of the Father. He comes off the cross, and calls the angels to destroy the people trying to kill Him! He gets justice, but what does it do to his ministry? He would not be the Savior of the world. He would not have the power to redeem us. He would never be referred to as the Redeemer of the world. He would not be proclaimed King of Kings or Lord of Hosts because he was not "obedient to death on the cross." He would not be exalted to the highest place and given the name above all names. We would be stuck without a Savior, needing to find a way into the family of God. Living with the Law, and not the liberty of the Spirit. Jesus Himself would have limited His own ministry if He had not forgiven. I am so glad He chose to forgive us, and die for us, and rise from the dead for us.

I am glad Philippians 2:1-11 is still in full force and not minimized by God's failure to forgive us.

> Therefore, if you have any encouragement from being united with Christ, if any comfort with his love, if any common sharing in the Spirit, if any tenderness and compassion, then make my joy complete by being like-minded, having the same love, being one in spirit and of one mind. Do nothing out of selfish ambition or vain conceit. Rather, in humility value others above yourselves, not looking to your own interest but each of you to the interest of others. In your relationships with one another,

have the same mindset as Christ Jesus: who being in very nature God, did not consider equality with God something to be used to his own advantage; rather, he made himself nothing by taking the very nature of a servant, being made in human likeness. And being found in appearance as man, he humbled himself as a man, by becoming obedient to death-- even death on a cross! Therefore, God exalted him to the highest place and gave him the name that is above every name, that at the name of Jesus every knee should bow, in heaven and on earth and under the earth, and every tongue acknowledge that Jesus Christ is Lord, to the glory of God the Father.

Let's review. If we don't forgive, then:

- We are not forgiven of our sins! This prevents us from going to heaven.
- Demons have Scriptural grounds to torture and torment us.
- We become like the person we don't forgive.
- We live in disobedience and remove ourselves from divine protection and peace.
- We try to get revenge and revenge is wrong.
- We end up in the prison we built for our offender.
- We limit the ministry God has for us.

Chapter Eight

How Do We Practice Biblical Forgiveness? We Practice Biblical Forgiveness By . . .

Understanding Christ Commands Us to Forgive!

I have studied the subject of forgiveness for over forty years. In all my studies, I can confirm one truth: Christ commands us to release people (forgive them) from the injury committed against us. Forgiveness is directly tied to love. God is love; therefore, since He is love, He is also forgiveness. It is the character of God to love and to forgive. So, when we decide to forgive people who have hurt and brutalized us, we begin to share in the very character of God. People are always saying, "I want to be more like Christ or God." Well, forgiveness is in fact placing you in a position to share in the image and character of God.

The world, or nonbelievers—for that matter, even believers— will take note that we have been with Jesus when we choose to forgive. We become the light and life to those around us. Because of our life, God is lifted up and glorified. To live in an unforgiving state is to take on the character of Satan. Some people I have met do not want to forgive. They want to know the other options. There are none. Forgiveness is a commandment. It is not a suggestion. It is not an option. To be an overcoming follower of Jesus Christ, forgiveness is the mandate. So please recognize, for the Christian, there is no alternative to forgiveness. It is the command that God gives us if we are His followers.

In addition to forgiving people, we may need to forgive a group or an entity. There are many people that hate and/or have un-forgiveness toward a political party, company, or government agency. If they have hurt you or done you wrong, then you must forgive. You are commanded to do so. Also, a word about perception: Some people could argue we were not hurt or that we weren't hurt that much, therefore, we don't need to forgive. Right or wrong, our perception becomes our reality. If we perceive someone has done us wrong, whether they have or not, we must forgive. Our perception is not always correct. However, it becomes our truth and therefore, if we believe someone has hurt us, we must forgive that person, group, or entity.

Chapter Nine

We Practice Biblical Forgiveness by Understanding Forgiveness is Not a One-Time Act.

Forgiveness is a Process!

T his truth is one of the most important revelations to understanding forgiveness. If we believe forgiveness is a one-time act, especially for major hurts and offenses, then we believe a lie. Forgiving others is a process that may require us to forgive that person, group, or entity hundreds of times (there is no set number). We must continue the process until we reach the state of forgiveness. That is when we know we are healed. There are three phases that need to be incorporated into our thinking and vocabulary:

1. The process of forgiveness
2. The state of forgiveness
3. The lifestyle of forgiveness

While you are forgiving someone, you are obviously in the process of forgiveness. You may have to forgive that person over and over, every time you remember the event, hurt, or brutalization, and you feel a negative emotion. It is a reminder from the Holy Spirit that you still need to forgive and are still in the process of forgiveness. Pray the forgiveness prayer at that moment. You should pray it out loud and with authority. It is the statement of obedience to Christ. It needs to be spoken out loud so that spiritual forces will know you are forgiving and you are choosing to be obedient to Jesus Christ.

The biblical mandate for this truth, "Forgiveness is a process" is found in Matthew 6:14-15. The Greek word used for forgiveness is a present tense verb that has ongoing action. So the idea Jesus expressed is for us to forgive and to continue to go on forgiving. This denotes the idea of a process. It has to be a process because we are human, and we can't forgive instantly like God does. Also, in the passage of the unforgiving forgiven servant, found in Matthew 18:22, Jesus states we must forgive 77 times or 7 x 70 (KJV) = 490 times, or an unlimited number of times, which denotes a process. So we don't forgive one time for the one event, but we forgive many times for the one event. In other words, every time the event is played out in our mind or emotions, we must choose to forgive.

The truth that is being stated above about forgiveness being a process and not a one-time act was an earth-shaking revelation for me personally. Prior to this truth, I believed forgiveness was something that worked for others, but not for me. I would forgive and then it felt like nothing happened. So I wrongly concluded that forgiveness didn't work for me. If you are an evil spirit or demon, this is a great lie to get people to embrace. This lie promotes the truth of needing to forgive and wanting to forgive and then forgiving, only to realize forgiveness doesn't work. However, it must work for others because it is a truth in God's Word. For me, the lie became a personal defeat in the area of forgiveness. I didn't think forgiveness worked for me. When I became aware of the truth that forgiveness is a process, I was set free to forgive.

I wrote earlier that we are in the process of forgiveness until we reach the state of forgiveness, which means we are healed and set free from the injury that has happened to us. The mechanism, or trigger point, that God uses to remind us to forgive is negative feelings or emotions that rise up in us when we remember the hurt or brutalization that we have suffered. Ironically, that is why people don't want to forgive, because they don't want to face the pain. Yet, that is the very thing God uses to signal us that we need to forgive.

When we face the pain, and choose to forgive, the pain is reduced and we begin to be healed. Also, the frequency of needing to forgive is reduced. Initially, we may have to forgive someone every ten to fifteen minutes. As we are faithful in practicing forgiveness, that time frame may increase to every thirty minutes, then once an hour, and then every two hours. Eventually it moves to three times a day, then twice a day, then once a day—you get the picture. In time, you will remember the terrible event as it happened, yet there will be no negative feeling or emotion attached to it. That is how you know you have completed the forgiveness process and are healed from the event. You have reached the state of forgiveness and it is *marvelous*! Once you reach this state, you are able to wish the person well who hurt and brutalized you. Then you will have fulfilled the passage of Scripture that calls you to love your enemy. The only way that this is accomplished is through forgiveness.

Years ago, I saw a couple at the funeral of a Christian pastor. These people had been helpful in starting the church that I have now pastored for many years. Well, after about a year-and-a-half of being a blessing, they left the church. I felt rejected and hurt by their decision to leave. They joined with two other families that almost destroyed the pioneer church that we had started. I began the process of choosing to forgive them and I completed the process. I was able to wish them well and had no negative feeling toward them. I had reached the state of forgiveness. When I went to a funeral and saw this Christian couple, which I had forgiven, my heart was filled with hate toward them. I was shocked. I had completed the process of forgiveness and now I became instantly unforgiving toward them.

All this negativity happened as we sang the first verse of "Amazing Grace." Inside I experienced amazing hate. I sent up a flare prayer to the Lord. I asked God, "What's going on?" God revealed to me during the second verse of "Amazing Grace" that since I had fallen out of forgiveness and back into un-forgiveness, that I needed to start choosing to forgive them again.

God said, "David, what do you do when you have un-forgiveness toward someone?"

I answered, "You start the process of forgiveness."

He said to me, "Then get to it."

So during the second and third verses, I chose to forgive them for the hurt they had sent my way. By the end of verse four, I had regained the state of forgiveness. This became a great learning moment for me. The forgiveness process must be implemented even if we have already become victorious but fall back. This gives credence to the idea that we stated earlier in this chapter; the lifestyle of forgiveness is a commitment to choose to begin forgiving immediately once we realize that we have un-forgiveness toward someone. No matter how mature we think we are, or how much forgiveness we have completed, if we fall back into un-forgiveness, the lifestyle of forgiveness dictates we begin the process of forgiveness again until we have completed it and once again attain the state of forgiveness.

Personal Insight

The more mature we are, the quicker we move to the process of forgiveness. The longer we choose not to forgive is proportionate to our immaturity.

Chapter Ten

We Practice Biblical Forgiveness By . . .

Understanding the Purpose God has For Our Emotional Pain

O ne of the many reasons people do not want to forgive is they don't want to bring up the past hurts and negative emotions that are associated with the terrible thing that happened to them. Why? It is painful! It is exhausting! It is easier, we think, just to let it stay buried. We also believe it is safer to not delve into these issues. Let sleeping dogs lie. However, the dogs are not sleeping. *God has a purpose for the pain.* The pain is our reminder to forgive. As long as we have emotional pain when we remember what we suffered, that is God's way of letting us know we need to forgive. If we have already begun the process of forgiveness, then that pain is a reminder that we need to continue forgiving. The pain becomes a mechanism, or God's trigger point, which informs us we have not reached the state of forgiveness. As we continue in the process of forgiveness, the emotional pain becomes less and less. That is how we know we are getting healed. Eventually, we wake up one day and find that we have been healed because we remember the event as it happened, and there is no negative feeling or emotion attached to it inside us. When the emotional pain associated with the event is gone, we know we have *completed* the process of forgiveness. This becomes a profound moment in our lives as we realize the weight and burden of un-forgiveness is gone and replaced with

God's profound blessing and love. As the chorus reads, "I traded my pain for the joy of the Lord." This sense of being set free by the truth of forgiveness has led some people to say, "I can't wait till I get hurt again, so I can forgive the person."

Now, let's not get crazy, but comments like that show me that un-forgiveness takes a terrible toll on our mind, body, soul, and spirit. When we forgive, we are being made into a new creation going forward in the sunlight of our Lord. It's a new day. We are free from the pain of the past. We have discovered for ourselves the biblical truth of John 8:32, "Then you will know the truth and the truth will set you free." John 8:36, "So if the Son sets you free, you will be free indeed." Remember, the Holy Spirit reminds us to forgive through emotional pain.

Chapter Eleven

We Practice Biblical Forgiveness By...

By Understanding Forgiveness is Not Based Upon Feelings, but on Our Choices.

F orgiveness is not based upon feelings, but on our choice! We live in a culture that worships feelings and emotions. The biggest lie that demons tell us is that forgiveness is a feeling and, by extension, if you don't feel like forgiving someone, you shouldn't have to; or that unless you feel the emotion of forgiveness (whatever that is), that you haven't forgiven your offender. Another lie is that if you don't feel the forgiveness, then you can't forgive. So many Christians get tripped up because they believe they don't have to forgive because they don't or won't feel it. Nothing could be further from the truth!

In addition to this lie, we also have another falsehood that has entered our culture and unfortunately the Christian mindset: "I have to be true to my feelings." Oh, really? That's like saying, "I have to be true to myself." Whatever we are true to, we end up serving. So do you want to serve your feelings and yourself? If you are going to be true to your feelings and serve them, and in doing so, serve yourself, you will not serve the Lord Jesus Christ. As Christians, we are not called to be true to our feelings or ourselves. We are called to be true to Christ. We are called to serve Him.

John 1:12 is a Scripture verse that every person should memorize: "Yet to all who received Him, to those who believe in His name,

He gave the right to become children of God." The word "right" is the Greek word *exousia*. In the King James Version, it is the word "power." It is the second word in the Greek New Testament that represents the word "power." It should not be confused with the word *dunamis*, from which comes our word for "dynamite." This word is associated with the Holy Spirit and His power or ability to do something. According to Strong's Concordance, *exousia* is defined as "the power to choose."[1] I would add "with God's moral authority or excellence." The power to choose is the greatest power we have as Christians. It is also directly related to forgiveness. Forgiveness is a choice we make to obey Christ regardless of the feelings we have inside of us.

An illustration of how *exousia* works is the police officer that is standing in the middle of an intersection directing traffic. When the officer holds up his hand with the palm facing out, all the traffic coming toward him stops. Cars, trucks, semis, buses, every vehicle stops because he has the moral authority to make them stop. His hand is not emitting some power that forces the vehicles to stop; it is the use of authority. If cars and trucks do not stop, the officer has friends he can radio ahead and they have the *dunamis* power to make vehicles stop, *dunamis* being the actual ability or power to do something.

So it is with us: we have the moral authority from God to make right choices. The authority we use to choose to serve Jesus cannot be defeated by any evil spirit or demon. The same is applied to choosing to forgive people who have hurt and brutalized us. Once we choose to forgive in the name of Jesus, no force of darkness can prevent us from doing so. Forgiveness becomes a choice, an act we choose to do by God's authority, His *exousia*, which is now in us. I believe this is how the Lord forgives us. He chooses to do so. Forgiveness is not a feeling, although positive feelings can come from it. At its core, forgiveness, like love, becomes a choice we make not based upon the other person's ability to perform.

I am describing *agape* love, which is God's love. The greatest act of love is sacrifice and forgiveness. It is imperative that we understand forgiveness is a choice and not a feeling. Many times, by our will, we obey first and positive feelings do follow righteous acts. Choice is so important that in the model Forgiveness Prayer, I have forgiveness listed as a statement of choice four times. The Forgiveness Prayer consists of just 108 words. Ninety-three of those words are phrases referencing the power of choosing to forgive. So no longer are we going to be lied to that forgiveness is a feeling. It is a choice; it is the power of choice that we have through Jesus, and we use it to forgive.

Jesus on the Cross

Jesus uttered the greatest forgiveness prayer on the cross as He was dying. "Father, forgive them for they don't know what they are doing." Jesus used His power of choice. I am sure that He didn't feel like forgiving us as He died a slow death of suffocation and a broken heart. But He did so because that is what mature love does. Remember, Jesus didn't want to go to the cross. He used His *exousia* to choose to drink from the cup, which He would have preferred to refuse. "Father, let this cup pass from me, nevertheless, your will be done."

Jesus in Heaven

Now Jesus is in heaven at the right hand of the Father, still staying, "Father, forgive them because they don't know what they are doing." When we sin, He is still faithful and loving. He chooses to love and forgive. His love and forgiveness are not based on our success or failure, but on His choice. Let us give praise and glory and honor to the Lord because He allows us to share in His *exousia* and thus have opportunity to become people of great maturity.

Chapter Twelve

We Can Practice Biblical Forgiveness By . . .

Understanding the Focus of Forgiveness is Not the Offender But is Christ Alone!

Many years ago, there was a young woman in California who came to her pastor because she could not forgive her grandfather. Her grandfather had molested her for a three-year period when she was nine, ten, and eleven. Understandably, she hated him for what he had done to her. Yet, she did see the benefit that forgiving him would bring into her life. She had been to my seminar on forgiveness and understood what to do, but she could not bring herself to forgive him.

The pastor was stumped. Here was a young lady who wanted to forgive the person who had devastated her life, but she couldn't bring herself to do it. When the pastor didn't get answers for people, he would ask the Lord to reveal the answer to him. He told her to give him two weeks to see what the Lord would reveal. During that two-week period, the Lord did speak to the pastor. He revealed that the reason she couldn't forgive her grandfather was that she had made him, the grandfather, the focus of her forgiveness. In her mind, he didn't deserve to be forgiven. The Lord spoke to the pastor that the focus of forgiveness is not our offender, but the Lord Himself. Jesus alone is the reason we forgive. When he shared this with her, she admitted it was true. She was then able to forgive her grandfather. She wanted to forgive her grandfather as an act of obedience and love for Jesus. She wanted to obey Jesus, so she forgave for Jesus.

Be aware that the offender usually doesn't want to be forgiven and does not deserve to be forgiven. In fact, I state this in the model Forgiveness Prayer. "I understand I forgive for Christ, not because my offender deserves it or wants it." Understanding this truth has become a great insight into why people won't or can't forgive. It has helped many people break through the un-forgiveness barrier and find the ability to forgive their offender.

Chapter Thirteen

We Practice Biblical Forgiveness By ...

Understanding Forgiveness Heals Us of the Emotional Pain that is Connected to Our Offense

Forgiveness heals us of the hurts that reside in our emotions. As we go through the process of forgiveness, we receive a small amount of healing. The emotional hurt associated with the offense diminishes every time we say the Forgiveness Prayer. We become less hurt, angry, or emotional. After saying the prayer ten times, we are better; after fifty times we are well, or are on our way to remembering the event as it happened, but now without the pain. Some people have taken a shortcut to stop the emotional pain in their lives. They edit what happened to them to the point that they alter the truth of what happened to them. They end up telling themselves a lie to rid themselves of the pain. The problem is they never get set free because it's the truth that sets us free. If we alter the truth, we can never be healed because we cannot address the real issue. In order for healing to occur, we must face the pain and the truth and let forgiveness bring healing into our lives.

Chapter Fourteen

Time for Review

If we release people (to forgive from Strong's Concordance means to "release or let go"[2]) from what they owe us, we let go of the debt they owe for hurting and brutalizing us. The injury (hurt) is not brought up in our emotions, thoughts, or outward behavior. If the injury keeps coming up, we need to continue releasing (forgiving). When in doubt, always forgive. Christ is saying to us today, that you can be released from the prison of un-forgiveness, bitterness, resentment, hate, and emotional murder. The key to getting out is hidden in Christ and His Word of forgiveness.

Recently, I was having a biblical forgiveness care session with a young woman who had been hurt by her mother. I lead her through the model Forgiveness Prayer, word for word. When we arrived at the point of the prayer where we state the offense, I led her in saying that her mother had "said hurtful and unkind words" to her. The first time through the prayer, she quoted me word for word. (I now take people through the prayer three times to jump-start their forgiveness process). The second time through, she changed the wording. When it came time to say "hurtful and unkind words," she said with earnest passion in her voice, as if reliving the painful moments, "I forgive my mom for calling me a bit**, a sl**, and a piece of sh**." (This young woman is different than the young woman in Chapter 4. Even though their stories are similar, they are different women with different stories.) Her language was real because the words had created a deep hurt in her. She sensed the release of forgiveness in her life and had a strong sense of God's peace flood over her. She was set free from the prison that Satan and his demons had created for her. The forces of evil thought they had a lifetime prison from the mother's cruel words. Praise be to God that she started the process of being set free by the power of biblical forgiveness, which is the forgiveness act spoken to us by Jesus Christ our Lord and God.

Chapter Fifteen

We Practice Biblical Forgiveness By...

Understanding that Carrying the Offense for Other People Does Not Justify Living in Un-forgiveness

Once you start practicing the lifestyle of forgiveness, you may think you have truly arrived to some level of spiritual truth and freedom, and you have! However, the demons that attack you with lies will not be taking a holiday. They have plans for you to continue to live in the prison of un-forgiveness. The backdoor to living in an unforgiving state is found in this lie called "carrying the offense for others" (friend, family member, colleague).

If the forces of darkness can trip us up, they will. They can get us to live in an un-forgiving state by getting us to have an unforgiving attitude toward someone who hurt or brutalized someone we like or love. We often feel justified in doing this because we don't see it as our sin of not forgiving. Yet, it is our sin. Please don't fall for this trick from the enemy of your soul. Not forgiving under any circumstances becomes our sin. If someone has hurt your friend, family, or anyone you care about, you must choose to forgive that person. People wrongly believe another lie concerning this matter of carrying the offense for someone else. They believe that carrying someone else's offense is a sign of loyalty to that person and that forgiving the offender is a sign of disloyalty to their friend or loved one. If it is a sign of loyalty, it is loyalty to a sin. People would never want to be loyal to a sin, but in this case, they feel their un-forgiveness is justified. Dear friends, do not fall for this trap. If you are married and someone hurts your spouse, you cannot carry the offense for him or her. Your spouse may feel like you're not being loyal to them. You cannot afford to be loyal to their offense and un-forgiveness. Help and encourage your spouse to come into the freedom of forgiveness.

Our children can provide opportunity to justify not forgiving, especially if someone has hurt or brutalized them. Don't fall for living in un-forgiveness under any circumstances. Make the hurt a teaching opportunity to show your child how to forgive. It will be a blessing to you and your child. Don't confuse forgiveness with anything else. We will talk more about this later in the book. We should not let people cross the line of respect into disrespecting us. Forgiveness does not mean you become a doormat for your offender. These are two different issues that are clearly separate and not meant to be joined together.

As a pastor, people come to me and tell me how someone has done me wrong and how they stood up for me. I thank the person for their loyalty, but caution them not to carry the offense against me as their own. As I have been saying, this is the backdoor to un-forgiveness. Don't allow this to entrap you. Sometimes folks are taken aback by my response. Listen, you carrying an offense for me is not going to please God. While it is well-meaning, it is wrong. Yes, it is good for you to support me, but don't let it carry you into un-forgiveness.

Chapter Sixteen

We Are Able to Practice Biblical Forgiveness By...

Understanding We Need to Forgive Ourselves Since Jesus Does

P aul is clear to us as Christians in the Book of Romans, "Therefore, there is now no condemnation to those that are in Christ Jesus" and also when Paul states, "He (Jesus) is faithful and just to cleanse us from all unrighteousness." These passages with the other Scriptures where Jesus forgave our sins, when combined together show us the power of Jesus forgiving us, releasing us from our sin, and commanding us to live free of condemnation. So, if Jesus is willing to forgive us, shouldn't we forgive ourselves?

Sometimes we are hardest on ourselves. Many people get involved in self-loathing. Why did I do such a stupid or terrible thing? My sins are too great or too many for God to use me. God can't use a cheat, or a murderer, or an adulterer, or a prostitute, or a deserter, or someone who abandons his or her family. Yet the Scripture has a list of sinners in Corinthians of whom we used to be and now we are in the family of God, being made into a new creation. The old way of living is melting away and the new person in Jesus Christ is being created. In forgiving oneself, we just plug our name into the model Forgiveness Prayer and list the offenses we have committed in the blank portion of the offense line and go through the Forgiveness Prayer.

Forgiveness Prayer Model for Forgiving Oneself

"In the name of Jesus Christ, I choose to forgive myself for (<u>list your wrongs, list everything and be as specific as possible</u>). I don't feel like I deserve to be forgiven, but I choose to do so out of obedience to Jesus Christ. I choose to forgive myself by my will because the Lord wants me to and I want to be more like Christ in every way."

Remember, forgiving oneself is a process just like forgiving someone else. Until we forgive ourselves, we cannot become the victorious Christian the Lord wants us to be.

Not forgiving oneself can go into two different extremes: self-loathing or pride. Either way we are so hurt by ourselves that our main problem is self-focus. Pride takes us to loving ourselves and attempting to believe we are never wrong. Well, no one is never wrong! Some people believe they are never wrong because they have been wrong so much they cannot accept being wrong one more time. In self-loathing, you are wrong all the time, so how can you ever be right in anything? The Lord wants us to come away from those two extreme positions and arrive to a perspective that is healthy.

Chapter Seventeen

We Practice Biblical Forgiveness By...

Understanding Forgiveness Does Not Acquit the Offender

I have talked to a number of people who have resisted the idea of forgiveness because they feel like it (forgiveness) is saying, "the person didn't hurt me, or offend me, or brutalize me. If I forgive, they get off scot free." It is this reasoning that has given permission to some to reject forgiveness and believe they are justified in doing so. They don't want to engage in an activity that nullifies their injury and the offense that was committed against them. This is all another deception that is perpetrated by those evil spirits who lie to us. The lie is designed for us to reject the message of forgiveness and the blessing that comes from its practice and lifestyle.

Here is the truth: forgiveness screams that our offender is guilty. Forgiveness by definition says, "you have done wrong to me." Otherwise, what is the point? If there were no offense, then there would be nothing to forgive. If there is an offense, then the person is guilty from our point of view and therefore must be released because he or she owes us for the hurt done to us.

Now a word about truth and perception: They don't always agree. The truth is what God knows and truth is what He is. Our perception becomes our truth, whether it is correct or not. If we believe we have been hurt, then we need to respond to that by choosing to forgive. If you are wronged from your perspective, you need to forgive. Forgiveness is always a great action in which to engage. You have an unlimited supply of forgiveness, so don't hesitate to use it.

If you believe you have been hurt, then you need to choose to forgive. Remember, forgiveness by definition means you have been injured; the offender is guilty, but must be released from the debt he owes you so that you can be released from prison.

Chapter Eighteen

We Practice Biblical Forgiveness By...

Understanding We Need to Forgive People, Groups, Organizations, Entities, and Even People Who Have Died

In 1974, as a young person, I heard Loren Cunningham share this story at a youth convention in San Diego. One night, the Lord woke up a pastor of a large church in Germany and said to him, "I am not going to answer any more of your prayers because you have an unforgiving heart."

The pastor thought about what the Lord had said and was puzzled. He could not figure out whom he had not forgiven! As he thought, the Word of the Lord came again to him and said the same thing, "I am not going to answer any more of your prayers because you have an unforgiving heart."

He continued to think and could not come up with whom he had not forgiven. The Lord repeated the statement a third time.

Finally, the man said, "Lord, who is it?"

The Lord answered, "You have not forgiven Adolf Hitler for what he did to Germany!"

The shocked pastor replied, "But Adolf Hitler is dead."

To which the Lord responded, "Not in your heart; he's very much alive."

Un-forgiveness is so powerful that it reaches from the grave to destroy our lives and relationships. Un-forgiveness is a terrible sin.

God hates it. It will rob you of God's blessing in your life. The Lord was not going to answer any more of this pastor's prayers because he had an unforgiving heart. You still need to forgive a person who has hurt or brutalized you, even though they may have passed. The injury is still inside of you and needs to be healed, and healing can only be attained through forgiveness.

Let us look at groups, organizations, businesses, governments, or any entity. If they have done you wrong or offended you or hurt you, you need to forgive. There are some people who hate political parties so much that they carry un-forgiveness in their heart. Listen, you do not want to have your sins remain un-forgiven by God. Do you want to take a chance of going to hell because you are mad at the Republicans or Democrats? Whatever party you think is taking America in a handbag to a certain place, may actually get you there for living in an unforgiving state over their terrible policies or positions. Maybe a business has done you wrong. Forgive them. Don't let an entity or a dead person hold you back from maturity and receiving God's blessing and healing.

Chapter Nineteen

We Practice Biblical Forgiveness By...

Understanding Forgiveness Heals Us So We Can Respond to New Offenses in a Mature Manner!

Forgiveness is such a power in our life. It changes all the dynamics and paradigms so that we can become more mature. Maturity is the ability to do the right thing in every situation. God is total maturity. He is able to do the right (righteous) choice/action in every situation. How amazing to never be wrong. That is God. When we don't understand what He is doing and why He is allowing us to suffer, He is working what is His good. We can trust Him to work the eternal good in every situation. Forgiveness gives us the ability to do the right thing, to see the greater good and do it. Oftentimes to do the right thing, we must sacrifice something in us or something we own. Maturity or immaturity always cost. One is an investment in eternal issues and the other is a divestment of eternal issues.

When we practice the lifestyle of forgiveness, it makes us enter into a style of living that God uses for His glory. Years ago on a mission trip, three pastors visited Malaysia and left the equivalent of $1,000 with a Malaysian pastor. They wanted him to buy land with this money. Each pastor left $333, which in those days translated into a total of 4,000 ringgits. The money was designated for a specific purpose. In addition, they had plans to raise $20,000 to build this Malaysian pastor a church in the provinces of Malaysia.

One church had already built him a small house on the church land that they purchased for him. The year before, they had planned to build a church with the $1,000 they left him to buy more land. During that year, the pastor in Malaysia had run low on food and used some of the designated money to buy rice to feed his family. Then, he spent more of the designated money on an honorarium for a visiting pastor. Then, the monsoon season was approaching and he had no windows in the house. His house would get about six inches of water in it because the rain would fall sideways from the force of the wind. He used the designated land money to buy some windows to keep the rain out of his house. Finally, he used the rest of the designated money to purchase furniture for his house because the windows now kept it dry. From January to January, in one year's time, all of this misappropriation of funds occurred.

When one of the pastors returned from the pastors' conference, he shared the terrible news of this pastor's mishandling of the money with the lead pastor. He then said, "I guess we won't be building this pastor a church because he is not trustworthy."

Before the lead pastor could say anything, God spoke to him and said, "1) the Malaysian pastor lives in abject poverty and you live in Disneyland; 2) If you were in his shoes, you would have probably done the same thing; and 3) Don't let the little thing Satan has done stop the great thing I want to do."

God spoke to the lead pastor to forgive the Malaysian pastor and go ahead and pay for the construction of the building, just don't let him handle the money. The $20,000 project mushroomed to $26,000. However, the Malaysian pastor oversaw the project (but not the money) and he brought the project in at $21,000. During the cement portion (floors, load-bearing brick columns) of the project, the monsoons were due to come. The pastors feared losing the cement they had purchased. The Malaysian pastor brought every bag of cement into his house which now had windows, and they didn't lose one bag of cement to the weather. What Satan meant for evil, God used for good. So dear friends, when you are wronged, God can turn things out for the good. People of maturity begin to look for the good He is doing. Remember, He promised He is working the good in every circumstance.

The truth of this chapter is forgiveness heals us so we can respond to new offenses in a mature manner! Normally when people steal from me, I want them to pay for their misdeed. That is the law. Usually, we live by the law. However, there is another law at work, it is the law of love. The law is usually the follow-up to our sins. The law imposes punishment. However, when the one who is wronged wants to disregard the "law" and put in its place the "law of love," forgiveness flows to the offender, then blessing, and then a chance to know mercy triumphs over judgment. The offender is not punished, but blessed, and in being blessed, he can now change to be a blessing. If this sounds familiar, it is. It's the way Jesus treats sinners. We deserve the punishment of the law, which is death (second death is hell). So we deserve hell. But the law of God which is the "law of love" sent the Son to the cross so that forgiveness would flow like a mighty river and mercy would triumph over judgment, so that we would not be punished with hell, but blessed with a new identity; the identity of "God as our Father, Jesus our elder brother, and a new destiny called eternal life, and a new home called heaven."

In the movie *Les Miserables*, the main character is a thief. After getting out of prison, he starts stealing again. He is caught by a police officer because he stole from the priest and the church. The officer takes the thief to the priest and asks if he had stolen articles of silver. The priest lies and says no. He turns to the thief and says, "You forgot the silver candlesticks I gave you."

The priest turned the situation of being sent back to a brutal forced labor prison into one of freedom. In doing so, he had freed the thief from his lifestyle of wrongdoing to become a man of blessing. Forgiveness gives us the ability to live out God's essence in us, "the law of love."

Chapter Twenty

Forgiveness Releases Us to New Levels of Ministry

When we engage in the "law of love," we may see miracles released in other people's lives. The Malaysian Pastor was released to a new level of ministry because the others forgave and blessed him. Anything he does for Christ, they get to share in because his ministry should have been disrupted, but instead it was released to move forward. His church has grown from fifty to 150. He held a youth conference and had 500 young people meeting in a building that was designed to seat 180 Malaysians (or 100 Americans). He won the mayor of his town to Jesus. He holds prayers in the mayor's office with the staff on Mondays. He has a radio ministry. He receives monthly financial support from the other pastors. He was elected head of the pastoral council of his area, because he has a building. He was released to a new level of ministry.

Chapter Twenty-One

We Practice Biblical Forgiveness By...

Understanding We Don't Go to Someone We are Forgiving and Tell Them We are Doing So

W hy, you may ask? Because you are setting yourself up to get hurt again. We are not talking about someone who has hurt or offended you coming to you to ask for forgiveness. That is a different scenario than what we are discussing here. If they come to you asking forgiveness, I hope you do extend it to that person. I hope you are already in the process or in the state of forgiveness. Over the years, people have made the great mistake of going to someone who hurt them and telling them they are forgiving them. Well, this usually turns into a nightmare. Your offender, many times, will blame you for what happened. When you say, "I just wanted to let you know I forgive you for what you did to me," oftentimes, they will respond by saying, "You forgive me? I should be the one to forgive you," and then they will proceed to hurt you again. It is not wise to open yourself up to this type of abuse.

Again, I reiterate, the focus of forgiveness is not the offender! The primary focus is Jesus! Secondly, the focus is you getting healed from the hurt and also from the sin of not forgiving. If you violate what I am sharing with you, you do so at your own heartache and peril. Listed below are some model scenarios and the correct responses:

Scenario	**Correct Response**
1. Someone hurt you and you want to tell him or her that you forgive him or her for what they did to you.	1. Don't do it! You will only be hurt again. They will accuse you of doing them wrong.
2. Someone hurt you and he/she is coming to you to acknowledge their wrongdoing and to ask you to forgive them.	2. Yes, forgive them! What option do you have as a follower of Jesus? Remember, forgiveness is a separate issue and should not be combined with other issues.
3. You have hurt or wronged someone. You are guilty! Go to them. Humble yourself and ask for forgiveness.	3. If they forgive you, great. If they don't, they will live with the terrible consequences of not forgiving.

Chapter Twenty-Two

We Practice Biblical Forgiveness By...

Rejecting the Lie That States We Should Only Forgive if Our Offender Comes to Us and Asks for Forgiveness

S imply put, this line of reasoning appears to be biblical, but it is not scripturally correct. It is based on the idea that Jesus requires us to ask first for forgiveness before He forgives us. Scripture states in 1 John 1:9, "When we ask Him to forgive us, He is faithful and just to forgive us from all unrighteousness." In this portion of Scripture, Jesus does not say that His forgiveness to us for sin is based upon us asking first. The passage is a testimony to us that when we do ask, He always forgives. Jesus is the "Great Forgiver." Any gift that comes from God is Him bestowing it upon us and not us earning it. We did not find God. God revealed Himself to us so we would find Him. We don't share in our salvation. It is a gift from God (not of works), so no one can boast that they have participated in saving themselves. Jesus bestowed forgiveness on all of us on the cross, when He said, "Father, forgive them for they don't know what they are doing." We do not activate forgiveness for our sins by asking for forgiveness. God activates forgiveness from His essence, which is love!

Forgiveness is not activated in our life by our offender. Forgiveness is activated by us choosing to obey Jesus. Then, as we forgive and live in the "law of love," we will begin to see the miracles it will produce.

Chapter Twenty-Three

❦

We Practice Biblical Forgiveness By...

Understanding We Do Not Forgive and Forget. We Do Forgive and Remember.

R ecently, I was in a time of ministry when I presented this simple truth. It was controversial for a few of the people and they began to resist the teaching. The perspective of the individuals was that to help them forgive, they also wanted to be able to forget. They felt they couldn't forgive unless they could also forget. How sad! They did not understand the tremendous healing power of forgiveness. Their assumption was the hurt or devastation they experienced was too painful to bear. In effect, they wanted to bury the memory of the negative event instead of getting healed from it. Remember, it is the nature of God to heal. He allows us to bury hurtful events as a coping mechanism. But what God wants for them is to remember and be healed. Forgiveness heals us of all negative emotions related to the hurt or devastation we have experienced.

So why do we forgive and not forget, but rather forgive and remember? If we don't remember the events of the past we will repeat the mistakes of the past. God never commands us to forget. He calls us to the truth. The truth sets us free. If someone has raped you or molested you or your child, you need to remember so you won't allow yourself to be victimized again by someone else or even by the same person.

God says forgiving and forgetting is His business. Paraphrased, Hebrews 8:12 reads, "He will remember our sins no more." Hebrews 8:12 is from Jeremiah 31:34, "For I will forgive their wickedness and remember their sins no more." Isaiah 43:25 reads, "I, even I, am He who blots out your transgressions, for my own sake, and will remember your sins no more." Forgiving and forgetting is reserved for God alone. Somehow He is able to do it. We should not or else we will repeat the mistakes of the past.

Conclusion

This book has dealt with the issue of understanding biblical forgiveness. Now it is time to forgive! The model Forgiveness Prayer from Chapter Four will be restated here in this portion of the book. When you forgive, please say it out loud. Read the prayer out loud. Read the prayer three times.

Forgiveness Prayer

1. In the name of Jesus Christ, I choose to forgive (<u>name of person</u>) for (<u>list offense or offenses</u>).
2. I don't feel like forgiving (<u>name of person</u>), but I choose to do so out of obedience to Jesus Christ.
3. I choose to forgive by my will because the Lord wants me to and I want to be more like Christ in every way!
4. I understand I forgive for Christ, not because (<u>name of person</u>) deserves it or wants it.
5. Since I am choosing to forgive, I affirm (<u>name of person</u>) did hurt me. He/She/They are guilty of hurting me, but through Christ, I choose to forgive him/her/them.

End of Forgiveness Prayer

If you are having trouble saying the prayer out loud, have someone you trust lead you in the prayer and you follow the script of the model prayer saying it out loud. I am constantly amazed at the number of people who have trouble saying the Forgiveness Prayer after they have concluded that they need to forgive. I guess it is another level of bondage that evil spirits have incorporated in their attack to keep us in un-forgiveness.

After you say the prayer, you may sense the burden of un-forgiveness is beginning to lift and you may feel a release in your inner self or a little lighter in your spirit or emotions. Sometime this happens to people.

Whether you feel something or not, you are beginning to get healed the first time you speak the prayer and mean it from your heart. You have started the process of forgiveness. Keep on forgiving until you reach the state of forgiveness and are healed, (such as remembering the terrible event and having no negative feeling or emotion remaining in you). You are able to wish your offender well and that they may find God and get their life straightened out so they can become healed as well.

Remember, it is the nature of God to heal everyone!

Bibliography

1. Strong, James. *Strong's Exhaustive Concordance of the Bible.* Nashville: Thomas Nelson, Inc., 1990.

2. Strong, James. *Strong's Exhaustive Concordance of the Bible.* Nashville: Thomas Nelson, Inc., 1990.

CPSIA information can be obtained
at www.ICGtesting.com
Printed in the USA
FFOW03n1855210518
46818256-48975FF